Kirk Cameron Ray Comfort

The Way of the Master for Kids

Teaching Kids How to Share Their Faith
Based on the Award-winning Television Series

genesis
PUBLISHING GROUP

Dedicated to:

Jack, Isabella, Julia, Summer, Danny, Robby, Luke, Ahna, James, Luke, and Olivia

The Way of the Master for Kids

Genesis Publishing Group
2002 Skyline Place
Bartlesville, OK 74006
www.genesis-group.net

Cover cartoons by Brad Snow (www.snowmedia.com)
Interior cartoons by Richard Gunther (richard@timaru.com) and Brad Snow
Edited by Lynn Copeland and Joette Whims
Design by Joe Potter (www.graphiks.com)
Printed in the United States of America
ISBN 0-9749300-5-9

Contents

Dear Parent:

As Christian parents, we all want our children to come to Christ, but how can we best play a part in making that a reality? And how can we then prepare our children to stand strong in their faith in spite of our secular culture? How do you answer their difficult questions about evolution, atheism, who made God, the reliability of the Bible, why suffering exists, etc.? Have you ever felt overwhelmed when trying to present biblical concepts to your children? Offering a concise, age-level explanation for the Bible's main teachings can be difficult. That's why we have written this book for you and your child.

These are the types of topics we discuss on our TV program, "The Way of the Master," in which we teach people how to share their faith biblically. We've presented this information in the same age-appropriate way that we share with our own children and grandchildren.

The Preschool Picture Book: The first section of this book, "God Loves the World," teaches preschoolers about God's love for them; about the sacrifice of His Son, Jesus Christ; and about God's Ten Rules—the Ten Commandments. As you read the story to your child and look at the pictures together, you will be able to help your child begin to understand God's wonderful plan of salvation. The story begins at creation and goes through the death and resurrection of Jesus.

As you read along, stop frequently to let your child express his or her thoughts about the pictures and then read the Bible verse under the picture. The verses are short so that your child can remember them. Young children love repetition, and as you read this story many times, encourage your child to memorize some of the verses.

The Primary-Age Book: Elementary children have different questions about life than preschoolers. Their knowledge and curiosity about the world are expanding through their school experiences. Sometimes they are confronted with difficult questions that you may find hard to answer. We have addressed a few of these questions in the next section, titled "Why, God?" In the first part of this section, they will find answers to these questions: "How do we know that God exists?" "Who made God?" "How do we know that the Bible is true?" "How do we know that evolution isn't true?" and "Why do bad things happen to people?" The second part of this section explains the importance of the Ten Commandments and presents a fun activity to help your child memorize the Ten Commandments and understand his or her need for the Savior.

The text is written simply enough that 6- to 10-year-olds can read the words. But you might want to read to your child, stopping frequently to answer questions and discuss the concepts. Either way, your child will be challenged to learn about God and his or her need of God's forgiveness, and to share those truths with others.

God bless you as you spend time with your child.

Kirk Cameron and Ray Comfort

God Loves the World

Ages 3 to 5

God made everything.

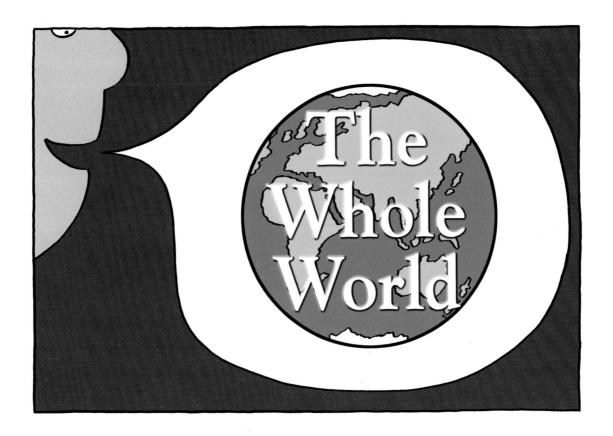

"In the beginning God created the heavens and the earth." (Genesis 1:1)

God created Adam and Eve.

"God created man in His own image." (Genesis 1:27)

They were very happy.

"God saw everything that He had made, and indeed it was very good."
(Genesis 1:31)

God gave them a rule. He said, "Do not eat of the fruit of this tree."

"Of the tree . . . you shall not eat." (Genesis 2:17)

Adam and Eve disobeyed God. They ate the fruit. (Disobeying God is called "sin.")

"[Eve] took of its fruit and ate. She also gave to her husband with her, and he ate." (Genesis 3:6)

Sin ruined everything. Because of sin, bad things happened.

"The whole creation groans and travails in pain." (Romans 8:22, CKJV)

God gave us the Ten Commandments to show us how we should live.

"These are the words which the LORD has commanded you to do."
(Exodus 35:1)

In the First Commandment, God says, "Love Me with all your heart."

"You shall love the LORD your God with all your heart." (Luke 10:27)

In another Commandment, God says, "Worship Me one day a week."

"Remember the Sabbath day, to keep it holy." (Exodus 20:8)

God also says, "Honor your parents."

"Honor your father and your mother." (Exodus 20:12)

In another Commandment, God tells us, "Do not steal."

"You shall not steal." (Exodus 20:15)

God also says, "Do not lie."

"You shall not . . . lie to one another." (Leviticus 19:11)

No matter how hard we try, we all break God's Commandments.

"All have sinned." (Romans 3:23)

Because God loves us so much, He made a way for us to be forgiven.

"God so loved the world that He gave His only begotten Son." (John 3:16)

God sent His Son into the world to be born as a baby.

"God sent forth His Son." (Galatians 4:4)

His name was Jesus.

"[Mary] will bring forth a Son, and you shall call His name JESUS."
(Matthew 1:21)

Jesus grew up. His parents were proud of Him.

"The Child grew and became strong in spirit, filled with wisdom."
(Luke 2:40)

Jesus always loved God and obeyed Him.

[Jesus said,] "I have kept My Father's commandments." (John 15:10)

He was very loving to others.

[Jesus said,] "As the Father loved Me, I also have loved you." (John 15:9)

Jesus did amazing things.
He walked on the water.

"Jesus went to them, walking on the sea." (Matthew 14:25)

He healed sick people.

"[Jesus] healed all who were sick." (Matthew 8:16)

He taught us more about God's Ten Commandments.

"Jesus said . . . , 'You shall love the LORD your God with all your heart.'"
(Matthew 22:37)

Jesus never broke God's Commandments —not even once. He never sinned.

"[Jesus] knew no sin." (2 Corinthians 5:21)

Remember, each of us has broken God's Commandments many times. We deserve to be punished. God's place of punishment is called Hell.

"The soul who sins shall die." (Ezekiel 18:4)

But Jesus took the punishment for our sins.

"God demonstrates His own love toward us, in that while we were still sinners, [Jesus] died for us." (Romans 5:8)

Jesus died for the whole world.

"[Jesus] died for all." (2 Corinthians 5:15)

Then He came back to life!

"Jesus Christ . . . was raised from the dead." (2 Timothy 2:8)

If we turn from our sins and trust Jesus, God will forgive us.

"Whoever believes in [Jesus] will receive [forgiveness] of sins." (Acts 10:43)

When we obey God's Commandments, we show that we love Him.

"If you love Me, keep My commandments." (John 14:15)

God will never leave you.

"[God] has said, 'I will never leave you.'" (Hebrews 13:5)

Jesus will be your Friend for life!

[Jesus said,] "I have called you friends." (John 15:15)

One day we can go to Heaven to live with God forever.

[Jesus said,] "In My Father's house are many mansions . . .
I go to prepare a place for you." (John 14:2)

"Why, God?"

Ages 6
and up

Hi, kids!

Do you have questions about God? Questions may have come up in school or in books that you don't know how to answer. What if someone says that God isn't real, or that the Bible isn't really true? Do you wonder who made God? How do we know where people came from? Why do bad things happen to people?

You may have seen us on our television show called "The Way of the Master." On our show, we talk to adults about God and the Bible and answer these same hard questions. This book was written to help you know the answers.

The second part of this book explains the importance of God's rules, the Ten Commandments. You will also find a fun activity to help you learn and obey the Ten Commandments. They will help you live your life in a way that pleases God. And you can use what you learn to help your friends know about God and His Son, Jesus.

Are you ready to tease your brain with these hard questions? We have invited a friend to help us explain the answers. His name is Albert Brainstein. So, now let's go take a closer look at these questions.

Kirk and Ray

Hi, kids!

My name is **Albert Brainstein**. I want to talk to you about some very important questions. As we look at the answers, you will see some Bible verses listed (they are in parentheses). Look up each verse in the Bible so that you can see what God says.

Here is our first question . . .

How do we know that God exists?

We can't see Him or touch Him.
(Read John 1:18.)

But you can know for sure that
God exists.

Let me tell you how.

Here is a famous painting.

How do you know
that there was a
painter?

The *painting* is proof that there was a painter. Paintings don't paint themselves.

You don't need to see the painter or touch him to know that he exists. You can know for sure that there was a painter *because you can see the painting!*

Here is creation.

How do we know that there is a God who created it?

Creation is proof that there is a Creator.
(Read Romans 1:20.)
Creation couldn't happen without a Creator.

You don't need to see God or touch Him to know that He exists. You can know for sure that there was a Creator *because you can see His creation!*

When we admire creation, we are really admiring the Creator, God.

Let's look closely at creation to see how wonderful the Creator is.

Think of the cow. God has made the cow so that it can eat green grass and its body will produce white milk. That's amazing. People can't make a machine to do that. Then people can turn the milk into cheese, butter, ice cream, or yogurt.

Think of the chicken. God has made the chicken so that it can eat wheat and worms and then produce delicious eggs that we can enjoy. We don't know how to do that. Therefore, Someone more intelligent than people made the chicken.

Think of the banana. It is shaped for your hand. It has a "tab" (like a soda can) and a wrapper that unzips. It's just the right shape for your mouth. It even curves toward your face to make it easy to eat. And it tastes good. It is clear that Someone made the banana especially for people (and monkeys) to eat.

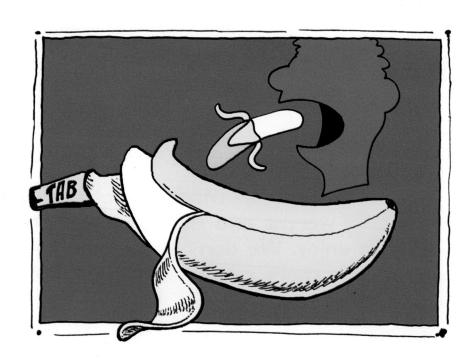

Think of the apple. It too is shaped for your hand. It has a groove for your thumb and one for your forefinger.
It tastes good

(you can eat the wrapper). It cleans your teeth, and it even has little seeds inside. If you put them in the ground, they grow into more apples. Someone made the apple especially for people (and horses) to eat.

Think of an ear of corn. You can eat it right off the cob. It can be made into cornbread. It can even be made into cornflakes and eaten for breakfast.

The banana, the apple, and the corn can be grown in the same garden, right next to each other. How does God make seeds that can grow into such different things, when they grow out of the same soil?

God's greatest creation was people. He especially created you. (Read Psalm 139:14.) Think of how wonderful your body is.

Look in a mirror. Notice all the parts of your face. Each part is especially made to help you live in your world.

Watch your eyes blink—if you can. They are more wonderfully made than any camera ever invented.

Listen to the sounds your ears are hearing.
See how your ears are shaped to catch the
sound and send it to your brain.

Now watch your mouth as you say some words.
How wonderfully God designed our mouths so
we can talk to
each other.

Then use your brain
to think about your
brain. It is much
more powerful than
any computer ever
invented.

The smartest scientist in the world can't create anything from nothing. He can only use things in God's creation to make other things. (Read Hebrews 3:4.) No one knows how to make a leaf or even a grain of sand from nothing— except God!

All around us, the wonders of creation show us how wonderful God, the Creator, is. (Read Psalm 19:1–3.) A person who says there is no God is not thinking properly. People call someone who doesn't believe in God an "atheist." God calls that person a "fool." (Read Psalm 14:1.)

Here is another
good question . . .

Who made God?

Here is the answer to this question: *Nobody.*
Nobody made God because He just always existed.
God didn't have a beginning.

The fact that God didn't have a beginning sounds strange to us because we live in "time." God lives in "eternity." Eternity means living forever and ever and ever. This fact is hard to understand, but it is true. Read these verses that tell us about God being eternal.

Psalm 90:2

Isaiah 57:15

Revelation 10:6

Can you count to a million? If you could, you would not even begin to count the amount of time in eternity. Eternity is like a ring. It goes around in a circle without a beginning or an end. That's how God is.

We are like a short piece of string. We have a beginning (we were born) and we will have an ending (we will die one day). But because God has no beginning and no end, He can rule over all creation with no problem. Take a minute to tell God how wonderful He is for being eternal!

Let's now look at another important question . . .

How do we know that the Bible is true?

The Bible is full of wonderful and miraculous stories. We can read about Jonah being swallowed by the big fish, Daniel staying alive in the lion's den, and Jesus walking on water. Could these stories be just made up, like fairy tales? Or did they really happen? Let's see if the Bible can be trusted.

The Bible is actually 66 books combined into one. About 40 different people wrote these books. God helped them do the writing. (Read 2 Timothy 3:16.) Here are some good reasons that prove God helped the writers. . .

The Bible contains many scientific facts that were written *thousands of years* before people discovered them. Here are a few:

- **The earth is round (Isaiah 40:22). (People used to think that the world was flat.)**

- **The earth floats in space (Job 26:7). (People once thought that something or someone was holding up the earth!)**

The Bible also contains medical facts that were written *thousands of years* before scientists proved that they are true. Here are some:

- **Hands should be washed in running water to remove invisible germs (Leviticus 15:13).**

- **Blood is the source of all life (Leviticus 17:11).**

The Bible also gives amazing prophecies. (A prophecy tells us what will happen in the future.) Here are some prophecies:

- The Bible said that the city of Tyre would be completely destroyed (Ezekiel 26:3,21). And it was.

- The Bible said that a king named Cyrus would rebuild the Jewish temple (Isaiah 44:28). And he did. The Bible tells us this hundreds of years before Cyrus was even born!

The Bible has many prophecies that tell us God would send His Son into the world. Hundreds of years before Jesus Christ, God's Son, was born, the Bible writers said:

- Christ would be born in Bethlehem (Micah 5:2).

- Christ would die a painful death (Psalm 22:16).

- Christ would rise from the dead (Psalm 16:10).

Jesus prophesied that the Jewish people would move back to their homeland (Israel) and into its capital city (Jerusalem). That didn't happen for 2,000 years. Then in 1967, this came true just like the Bible said it would!

Only God could have known in advance that all these things would happen. This proves that the men who wrote the Bible were helped by God. Because God helped to write the Bible, we can trust that all its words are true. It is impossible for God to lie. (Read Hebrews 6:18.)

Some people say that the Bible has changed since it was written. But in 1949, some scrolls were found near the Dead Sea in Israel. (Scrolls are rolled up pieces of paper.) These scrolls were large parts of the Bible that were written thousands of years ago. When they were compared to the modern Bible, the words were the same. How amazing that the Bible hasn't changed in all those years! The Bible is still the world's best-selling book. People read it all over the world.

If you believe that the Bible is true, you are in good company. Many famous people believed the Bible too. That includes George Washington, Abraham Lincoln, Thomas Jefferson, Teddy Roosevelt, Ronald Reagan, and many others.

Some people, though, don't believe the Bible is true. They don't believe that God made all of creation. Instead, they believe in something called "evolution."

So here is another important question . . .

How do we know that evolution isn't true?

Way back in the 1800s, a man named Charles Darwin had an idea. He thought that perhaps people were not created by God like the Bible says. He decided that people came from monkeys. He even wrote a book about his idea, called *The Origin of Species*. Mr. Darwin's idea is known as the theory (idea) of evolution. The word "evolution" means "change."

The Bible says that the first people were Adam and Eve—and that God created them as people, not monkeys. But evolution says that monkeys changed into people over millions of years. Both ideas cannot be

right. Which one is true? When Mr. Darwin's book was printed, many people stopped believing in the Bible and believed in evolution instead.

Some scientists thought up more ideas about evolution that made evolution seem true. They said that bones they had dug up out of the ground proved that Mr. Darwin was right.

In 1912, someone found a piece of a skull and a jawbone that looked like part man and part monkey. The people who believed in evolution thought this proved that people came from monkeys. They said it was the "missing link." They called this discovery "Piltdown Man" and said it was a million years old. The evolution scientists were excited. They thought it proved that the Bible was wrong.

Then, in 1953, scientists discovered that "Piltdown Man" was a trick. The skull was only 600 years old. The jawbone was 500 years old—and it really came from a monkey, not from a man.[1]

Other scientists dug up a single *tooth* and called this discovery "Nebraska Man." They thought *this* was the "missing link." But it was discovered later that this was also a trick. It was just a tooth from a pig!

Many other bones have been discovered that some people said were proof of Mr. Darwin's idea, but they have all turned out to be hoaxes[2] (tricks).

Some people still think that evolution is true. They even draw pictures of monkeys turning into men, to try to convince people that it happened. But no one has any proof. Some scientists say that Mr. Darwin's idea is just a "fairy tale for grown-ups."[3] They say that people who tell us that evolution is true are really "con-men"[4] (liars).

How silly to believe that people came from monkeys! **The Bible teaches us that all creatures have babies that are just like the parents. (Read Genesis 1:24.) You can see that this is true everywhere you look. Dogs don't have kittens; they have puppies. Sheep don't have puppies; they have lambs. Pigs have piglets. Fish have fish. Monkeys have baby monkeys—not people! (Read 1 Corinthians 15:39.)**

After all these years, scientists *still* have not found Mr. Darwin's "missing link" to prove that people came from monkeys. No one can prove evolution . . . because it is not true.[5] But it is easy to prove that

the Bible is true. We can just look around us everywhere and see that God has created the earth with beauty and wonder.

The Bible tells us about our world. It even gives us the answer to our next question . . .

Why do bad things happen to people?

Our world has lots of problems. People get sick. They get hurt in terrible earthquakes, tornadoes, hurricanes, floods, and blizzards. Accidents happen everywhere.

But things weren't always this way.

When God created Adam and Eve, everything was wonderful. They didn't have to worry about getting sick or hurt. They had lots of food and were happy.

But then they sinned. (Sin is disobeying God.) When they sinned, many bad things started to happen in the world.

But God says that, one day, all those who truly love Him will get to go to a place called Heaven. In Heaven, people won't feel pain or sadness anymore. There will be no more earthquakes or floods or other disasters. Won't that be a wonderful place?

The people who love and obey God will get to enjoy this wonderful place. Does this describe you? We show that we love God by obeying what He says in His Word, the Bible. Read these verses to see how important it is to obey God.

Exodus 19:5

Deuteronomy 27:10

Acts 5:29

Are you a genius?

In the Bible, God gives us rules that He wants us to obey. The most important rules are the **Ten Commandments**. You can read the **Ten Commandments** in Exodus 20:1–17.

Now we are **going** to test your memory to see if you are a genius!

TEST NUMBER ONE

Let's see if you can memorize the Ten Commandments. We will list each Commandment. You will see a picture next to each one to help you remember them.[6]

Put the pictures in your mind, and they will remind you of each Commandment. Then test your memory, and grade yourself.

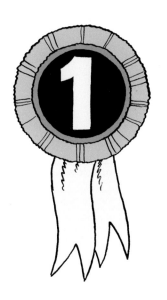

1. "You shall have no other gods before Me."
(God should be Number One.)

2. "You shall not make yourself any graven image."
(Don't bow down to anything but God.)

3. **"You shall not take the name of the Lord your God in vain."**
(Don't use your lips to dishonor God.)

4. **"Remember the Sabbath Day to keep it holy."**
(Don't neglect the things of God.)

5. "Honor your father and your mother."

6. "You shall not kill."

7. "You shall not commit adultery."
(Adultery leaves a broken heart.)

8. "You shall not steal."

9. "You shall not lie."
(a "lying" nine)

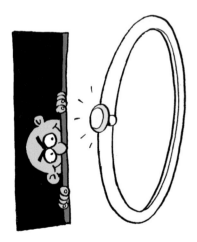

10. "You shall not covet."
(want what others have)

Now, get a pencil . . .

. . . and check your memory.

What is number . . . ?

10 _____

_____

9 _____

_____

8 _____

_____

7 _____

_____

6 _____

_____

And what is number . . . ?

5 _____

_____

4 _____

_____

3 _____

_____

2 _____

_____

1 _____

_____

If you remembered five, you did okay . . .
but you need to try again.

Six: You did well.

    Seven: Good.

        Eight: Very good.

            Nine: Wonderful!

Ten: You're a **genius!**

TEST NUMBER TWO

Why do you think that God gave us the **Ten Commandments?**

A As a way to get to Heaven?

B As a mirror to look into?

If you chose "A" you are

~~pong~~

~~wronge~~

wrong

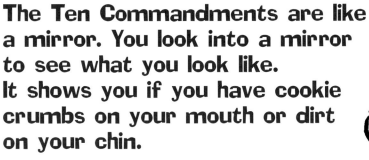

The Ten Commandments are like a mirror. You look into a mirror to see what you look like.
It shows you if you have cookie crumbs on your mouth or dirt on your chin.

In the same way, we **don't know** how bad our behavior is until we look into God's "mirror," the Ten Commandments. They show us what we are **doing wrong**.

Let's look into them:

Do you remember number 9? What is it?
Have you ever lied to anyone?

How about number 5?
Have you always obeyed your parents?

What about number 6?
The Bible says if you hate someone,
you've committed murder.

Have you always loved God? (Number 1)

Have you ever stolen something? (Number 8)

Have you ever been greedy? (Number 10)

Do you see how the Commandments act like a mirror? Did they help you understand what you have done wrong? The Ten Commandments show us how bad we are and that we need to be made clean.

One day we will see God. He will judge us by whether we have obeyed His Commandments.

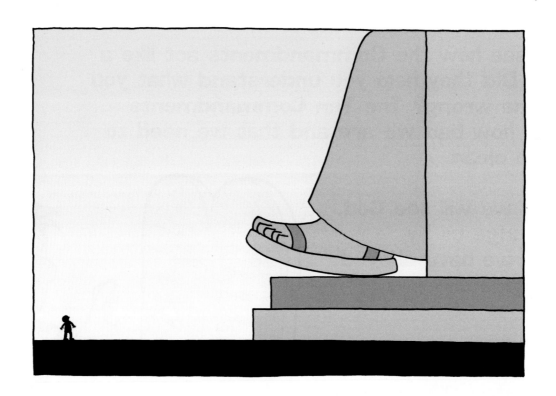

On that day, called the **Day of Judgment**, God will punish people who have broken the **Ten Commandments**.

Those people will be sent to a place called **Hell**.
God doesn't want anyone to go there. It is a terrible place of punishment.

God doesn't want you
to be punished.

He loves you so much that He
made a way for you to be clean
before **Judgment Day.**

To see what a wonderful thing God did so we could become clean, listen to this story.

A man had a son who was really bad. He did many bad things, including lying and stealing, and found himself in trouble with the police.

THE LONG ARM OF THE LAW

The son had to face a judge for his crime. The judge said he had to pay a $50,000 fine or go to jail. The son didn't have any money to pay the fine, so the judge was about to send him to prison.

Then the father stepped forward and said he would pay the fine for his son. The amount of money was so high that it took all the father's life's savings. But now the son didn't have to go to prison.

This shows how much the father loved his son.

We are like that son. We have done many wrong things and deserve to be punished.

But God sent His Son Jesus to earth to take the punishment for our sins. Jesus took our punishment by dying on a cross. Then He rose from the dead.

Because Jesus took our punishment for us, that means we don't have to be punished by God. God will forgive us so we can live with Him forever!

Isn't it amazing how much God loves us!

Maybe you see that you need to be clean and you want to receive God's forgiveness. What should you do?

Ask God to forgive you for the Commandments you have broken. Then tell Jesus that you want to serve Him and obey God in everything you do.

You can read Psalm 51, and use it like a prayer to talk to God. Or you might want to say a prayer like this. But the words aren't important. What matters to God is what's in your heart. You must really mean what you say to God.

Dear God,

I have broken many of Your Commandments. I am very sorry.
I believe that Jesus died on the cross to pay for my sins. Please forgive my sins and make me clean. Help me to obey Your commands. Thank You so much. Amen.

God promises, "I will never leave you" (Hebrews 13:5). You can count on Him to always be with you—in good times and in bad times. Thank Him often for being your closest Friend.

Read your Bible every day. It is full of exciting stories. Begin by reading the Book of John, and obey what you read.

We have looked at some important questions. Now that you know how to answer these questions, you can tell your friends what you have learned. They will want to know about God and the Bible, and about God's love for them too.

1. First, think of some friends who don't know about God like you do. Write down their names.

_____

_____

2. Pray. Ask God to help you say the right words to your friends.

3. Show them how the Ten Commandments are like a mirror to help us see what we are doing wrong. (Help them take the Ten Commandments test in this book.)

4. Tell them that Jesus died to take the punishment for their sins. Explain that they need God to make them clean and to forgive them for the wrong things they have done, or else they will be punished in a place called Hell.

5. Help them read the pages in this book that tell how to ask God for His forgiveness.

6. Encourage your friend to read the Bible every day, and obey it.

We thank God for you. You are in our prayers. We are so glad that you have learned about God's love and forgiveness. It's an exciting life when we live for God.

Yours faithfully,

Kirk and Ray

Notes:

1. *Our Times: The Illustrated History of the 20th Century* (Turner Publishing, 1995), 94.
2. See *The Evidence Bible* compiled by Ray Comfort (Bridge-Logos Publishers, 2001).
3. Professor Louis Bounoure, Director of Research, National Center of Scientific Research.
4. Dr. T. N. Tahmisian, Atomic Energy Commission, USA.
5. See the episode "Evolution" from "The Way of the Master" series.
6. See the episode "How to Witness to a Family Member" from "The Way of the Master" series, which has this test in animated form.

For more books, tracts, videos, DVDs, and tapes
by Kirk Cameron and Ray Comfort, see
www.wayofthemaster.com

or call The Way of the Master Ministries
877-496-8688